THE WORLD OF SKATEBOARDING

THE COMPLETE BOOK OF SKATEBOARDS AND SKATEBOARDING GEAR

Brian Wingate

the rosen publishing group's
rosen
central

Published in 2003 by the Rosen Publishing Group, Inc.
29 East 21st Street, New York, NY 10010

Library of Congress Cataloging-in-Publication Data

Wingate, Brian.
The complete book of skateboards and skateboarding gear / By
Brian Wingate.
    p. cm. — (The world of skateboarding)
Includes bibliographical references (p.   ) and index.
ISBN 0-8239-3648-1 (library binding)
1. Skateboards. 2. Skateboarding—Equipment and supplies. I.
Title. II. Series.
GV859.8 .W57 2003
796.22—dc21
                                                              2002003759

Manufactured in the United States of America

CONTENTS

INTRODUCTION

So you want to ride a skateboard! You've seen your friends kicking cool tricks and you've seen Tony Hawk and other skate stars tearing up the screen on television and in video games. They make it look easy. You could just jump on your board and ride away, right? Well, it's not that simple. For one thing, the pros you see on television and at skate contests have practiced for thousands of hours to make their tricks look so easy. Skateboarding is a vibrant sport. There's a lot to learn when you're getting started, and sometimes it's a lot to wrap your head around. Does that mean it's like going to school? No, but just like going to school, learning can be fun.

If you really want to skate, you must know where to start. This will be your one-stop education station. New to the sport? That's OK. By the time we're done you'll be able to walk into a skateboard shop

Everyone, especially young beginners, needs to wear protective gear when learning how to skateboard.

knowing what you need. In these pages you will find the answers to the questions that any beginning skater will ask: How do I choose a board? How do I take care of it? Are some boards better than others? How many are there to choose from? And that most important of questions: What should I wear? You'll also learn how to protect your body so you can skate for many years.

So let's start our skateboard tour. Before you jump on that board, let's start at the beginning of the sport. Step back in time for a moment and we'll learn about the birth of skateboarding.

The sport of skateboarding has come a long way. The first commercial skateboard hit the market in 1959. Before that, kids all across the country had to take apart roller skates and nail the metal wheels to the bottom of a piece of wood. Those old metal wheels were loud and bumpy even on smooth pavement. And when you wanted to turn you had to get off your board, point it in a new direction, and hop on again.

Surf's Up

Skip ahead a few years to the early 1960s. Surfing was king in California. Thousands of surfers turned out every day to catch the great waves rolling in on the California coast. The waves there are some of the best in the world, but some days even those waves are flat. Some surfers got the bright idea that if they couldn't surf the waves on those days, they were going to surf the pavement.

How could they surf the pavement? You got it—with skateboards. But it was hard to surf anything with roller skate wheels because those metal wheels were just too loud and clunky.

New Directions

Soon new inventions began popping up in the skateboard world. Skate manufacturers started making wheels out of hard clay. They were much better than the metal wheels, but they still had their drawbacks. The clay wheels didn't grip the road very well, so many skaters were taking dangerous falls. Pebbles and stones could get stuck in the wheels and jam the board. The rider would go flying off in the middle of the ride. Parents and lawmakers got pretty upset about this new craze. By the end of 1965, skateboarding had almost disappeared.

Barefoot Frenzy

If you see pictures of some of the "sidewalk surfers" in the early 1960s, you will notice something very strange about them. Take a long look. That's right— THEY'RE NOT WEARING ANY SHOES. That seems like a crazy thought now, but these skaters thought it was only natural to go barefoot when they "surfed" on land. Skateboard safety has improved a lot since those days.

A group of kids skate down a street in 1965, shortly before skateboarding fell off the map for a long time.

Going Underground

Such a great sport was not going to die so easily. Skaters may not have been visible everywhere, but they were still around. Those who truly loved the sport went underground and continued to skate. They skated in drained pools and city drainage ditches.

In the 1970s, a new wheel was invented that brought the sport back into the spotlight. Frank Nasworthy developed the urethane wheel, a plastic wheel that was much softer and quieter than clay. Skaters didn't have to worry about flying off the board anymore and getting a mouthful of dirt. The new plastic wheels glided over pebbles and stones. Now more skaters hit the streets, and the sport evolved.

The style of skating was different back then. Many boards were made of fiberglass, which made them very flexible. Slalom, a contest in which skaters weave in and out of cones and other obstacles while skating at high speeds, was very popular.

The skaters using the drained pools were laying the foundation for the more technical skating that we see today. At first they just carved the pool, but gradually some skaters started to do tricks above the lip. The early handstands and grabs at the edge of the pool were the birth of vert as we know it. As more skaters took their tricks above the rim, vert ramps started popping up in backyards and parks across the country.

The 1980s and 1990s

Vert and freestyle took center stage throughout the early 1980s, and new stars like Tony Hawk and Rodney Mullen dominated contests. Streetstyle skating was starting to gain momentum, and by the late '80s, street skating was the rage.

Everybody took a hit in the early 1990s. The skateboard industry struggled along with the rest of the national economy and suffered from the growing popularity of in-line skating. But by 1995, the X Games on ESPN introduced the joys of skateboarding to an entirely new audience, and skateboard fever was reborn across the world.

The sport hasn't looked back since. Hundreds of skateparks are springing up every year, and each one seems better than the last. Skateboarders are on television and in video games. It looks

Colin McKay gets some air at the X Games, which introduced the sport to a whole new generation.

like the sport is here to stay, especially since thousands of kids pick up a board every day for the first time.

And now you're ready to join them. Hundreds of skate companies are ready to meet your every need. The question is—what *do* you need? Let's find out.

OK, you're ready to get your own board and get started. But now that you're ready to get a board, you probably have a few questions. Questions like "What do I need to know before I buy a board?" and "Are all boards the same?" To answer these questions, we need a tour of skateboard biology.

Deck

The board (also called a blank or a deck) is your takeoff platform. Boards come in a variety of sizes and materials. What works best for you depends on your size, weight, skill level, and type of skating.

Feet First

Let's start at the bottom—your feet. If you have big feet, you'll need a wider board. You don't want your toes hanging too far off the side while you're in the air. You want your board to be solid and supportive underneath you. Most boards today are between 7.5 and 8 inches wide. You can always find some exceptions.

Board Length

Decks come in different lengths, and you can pick what size you want based on your own preference. Most boards today are between 31 and 32.5 inches long. If you want to freestyle like Rodney Mullen, then you should pick up a shorter board. A shorter board gives you more control. You'll be able to spin faster and make tight turns. If you're tackling the vert ramps like Tony Hawk, pick up a longer board with more width for stability. The 31-inch

Ask Around!

If you're getting confused with all these measurements, don't worry too much. We talked with several skaters and asked them to share their experiences and advice with us. We'll hear from some of them throughout the book. Andre Jarreau is seventeen years old and has been skating for six years. Andre says, "If you want to start skating, get a skateboard. That's all. You can start anywhere. There's no need to go out and spend 120 bucks on a board when you first start skating. Just keep pushing around until you feel what's right for you and you can adjust your board accordingly."

board is a good place to start. If you're very tall or heavy, get a longer and wider board because it will fully support your weight.

Most boards these days are made of seven-ply maple. That means that seven layers (plies) of maple wood are pressed together and glued tightly. Most people agree that seven-ply maple boards give a strong surface that still has some flexibility.

Some boards are more flexible than others. When you're just getting started, you'll probably want a nice, firm surface beneath your feet, so get a board with less flex. This helps you get

Board lengths can vary greatly, including special long boards like the one pictured here.

used to the motion of the skateboard. As you improve you'll want to try boards with a little more flex. Most pros use very flexible boards.

Concave

Another aspect of your deck is its concavity. That's the amount of upward curve in the sides of the deck. A completely flat board has no concavity. A board with a lot of concavity dips slightly in the middle and rises on the sides. Most skaters say that greater concavity helps their feet get a grip on the deck and also helps flip the board faster. You'll have to find out what feels right for you and adjust as you go. Skater Andre Jarreau says, "I liked a skinny board with lots of concave but now I like big wide boards with just a little bit of concave. After I came into my own out here in the park I felt it [less concavity] was better. Anything else feels weird now."

Get a Grip!

Make sure you have some grip on that board! Remember, your feet can slip off the board while you're flying through the air. Put some grip tape on the top of the board so your shoes have something to hold onto, even if that means covering up some cool art. Grip tape works just like a sticker—you peel off the backing and apply it directly to your board. Many skaters cover the entire tops of their boards with grip tape so that their feet will always have something to grab onto. You can buy grip tape cheaply at any skate shop.

Board Brands

In the mid 1990s, skateboard companies popped up everywhere. Today, you can buy from hundreds of skate companies around the world. The question is always the same: What feels right for you? Everyone says that he or she has the best product, but it's up to you to decide that for yourself.

There are literally hundreds, if not thousands, of different skateboards on the market to choose from.

Wheels

A board won't go anywhere without wheels. All of the wheels on skateboards today are made of urethane, a kind of durable plastic. Urethane seems to make the perfect skateboard wheel because it lasts for a very long time and doesn't lose its shape. The loud metal wheels and hard clay wheels of early boards are

You can buy a deck from any of these companies online at Skateboard.com:

Alien Workshop	Enjoi	Phantom
Baker	The Firm	Pig
Birdhouse	Flip	Real
Black Label	Foundation	Rhino
Blind	Girl	Santa Cruz
Chocolate	Habitat	Shorty's
Darkstar	Hollywood	Toy Machine
Deca	Hook-Ups	World Industries
DNA	Maple	Zero
Dynasty	New Deal	
Element	151	

now a thing of the past. With urethane wheels, you can ride on almost any surface. Just be careful not to ride on a wet surface because urethane wheels get pretty slippery.

Diameters and Durometers

You can get wheels in a variety of sizes and softness. The size of a wheel is listed as the wheel's diameter in millimeters.

There is quite a range in wheel sizes, but most are between 50 and 65 millimeters. The hardness of a wheel is measured with a gadget called a durometer. The durometer rates the hardness of a wheel based on a numerical scale—the higher the number, the harder the wheel.

If you're just getting started, a wider and softer set of wheels is for you. That's because softer wheels give you a smoother ride, and more width gives you better balance. Ramp skaters like wide, hard wheels because the width gives stability and the hardness gives good speed on the ramp.

Wheels come in a variety of sizes and degrees of hardness.

As your skills and balance improve, you can move up to harder wheels that will increase your speed. Just be sure to pick a wheel size and softness that is appropriate for your skill level. If you're skating ramps, those hard wheels are going to rattle your knees if you then decide to ride on street pavement. You'll want to put on some softer wheels that absorb more of the shock from the road. Wheels with a hardness of 95a (durometer reading) usually work well both on ramps and rougher terrain.

Get Your Bearings

A wheel doesn't spin without bearings. Bearings are the little round metal balls that help the wheel spin smoothly around the truck axle. A better bearing gives you a faster ride. Many wheel bearings today are encased in a sleeve (it looks like a fat, wide washer). The sleeve keeps out dirt and water.

Choosing Your Wheel

Here's an insider tip when you're picking your gear: Wheels come with all kinds of designs on them, but be sure to get some that have the designs on the outside. The inside of the wheel should still be a clear whitish color. This is the natural color of urethane. Exploratorium, on the Web at www.exploratorium.edu/skateboarding/skatedesignwheel.html, notes that when dyes and pigments are injected into the wheels to give them color, the chemical makeup of the wheel itself is changed. Urethane loses some of its strength when it is altered by dyes and pigments.

Trucks

Without the trucks, your wheels would fall off. Trucks are the metal units that hold your wheels onto the board. The axles of the wheels go through the trucks. They also provide some cushion and allow you to turn the board. Some people prefer their trucks to

Wheels online at Skateboard.com:

Alien Workshop	The Firm	Rhino
Baker	Flip	Ricta
Birdhouse	Foundation	Speed Demons
Black Label	Ghetto Child	Spitfire
Blind	Habitat	Super Imperial
Darkstar	Hollywood	Toy Machine
Deca	Hook-Ups	World Industries
DNA	Maple	Zero
Dynasty	151	
Element	Pig Wheels	

have a lot of "give," while others prefer a really tight ride. You'll have to see what feels right to you.

If you have friends that skate, ask to ride their boards and see how they feel. Try a board with tight trucks and then one with loose trucks. Which feels better to you? Trust your judgment. Many skaters swear that the trucks on their board make a big difference in the quality of their ride. Poorly made trucks are heavy and may fall apart easily. You want trucks that are lightweight, but strong and safe enough to withstand a lot of skater abuse.

Trucks Broken Down

Trucks are made of several different parts. The base plate is the part that attaches directly to the deck. The bolt that comes through the base plate sounds important, and it is. It's called the kingpin. You can adjust this bolt to make your trucks looser or tighter. This works because the kingpin clamps down on the bushings, which control the amount of pivot that you have when leaning left or right. They are also called pivot bushings. Last but not least, the hangar is the metal part that protects the axle and locks around the kingpin and bushings. When you grind a curb you are riding on the hangar. Trucks are made of metal and are therefore durable. You can pretty much grind on any surface over and over for a long time before they wear out. Just make sure you keep all bolts to the deck tight.

Trucks can be adjusted by turning the kingpin to make them looser or tighter.

The Next Level

In the past few years, trucks have gotten more specialized. Tensor Trucks offers a plastic grind plate to help with those nose slides and tail slides. Some boast about their lighter composition while others

Trucks online at Skateboard.com:

Destroyer	Phantom
Destructo	Royal
GrindKing	Ruckus
Independent	Tensor
Krux	Venture
Monster	World Industries

stress their durability. Whether they are marketed as "lightweight" or "heavy duty," most trucks still weigh between ten and thirteen ounces.

Some companies offer high or low trucks. Andre Jarreau shared his thoughts on the choice of high versus low trucks: "I think you can ollie higher with bigger trucks. I definitely feel like I can get more air, especially out of a quarter pipe, with higher trucks. People who want lower trucks are more into technical skating, like switch flips, flips into grinds, and flips out of grinds. When it's closer to the ground, it seems that you have more control. And people who do that tend to have tighter bushings, too."

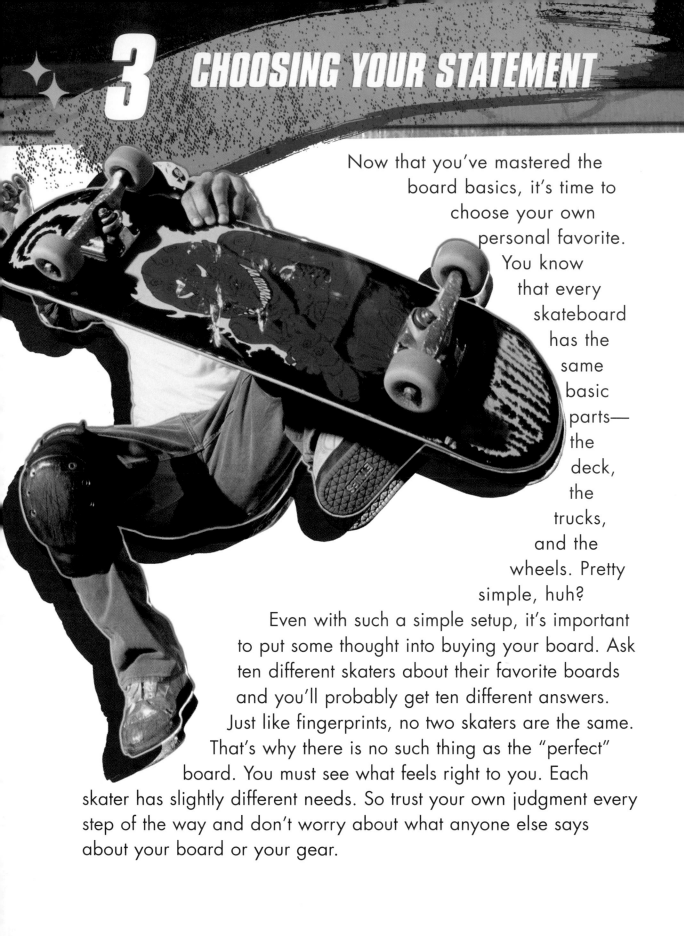

3 CHOOSING YOUR STATEMENT

Now that you've mastered the board basics, it's time to choose your own personal favorite. You know that every skateboard has the same basic parts—the deck, the trucks, and the wheels. Pretty simple, huh?

Even with such a simple setup, it's important to put some thought into buying your board. Ask ten different skaters about their favorite boards and you'll probably get ten different answers. Just like fingerprints, no two skaters are the same. That's why there is no such thing as the "perfect" board. You must see what feels right to you. Each skater has slightly different needs. So trust your own judgment every step of the way and don't worry about what anyone else says about your board or your gear.

So Many Boards, So Little Time

If you've ever been in a skateboard shop, you know that picking a board is not always an easy decision. There are hundreds of designs available on the shelves. You go into a skate shop and dozens of boards line the walls. It's overwhelming to say the least! Where do you begin?

Shopping for a board can be like a magic recipe. Throw in a little bit of this and a little bit of that, and eventually you find the perfect combination that feels just right for you. Make your own statement. You can even buy a board with no art—a blank—and paint it yourself. Be your own pro.

For many skaters, their board is a form of self-expression. Others like to buy the board that their favorite skater uses. Most pro skaters have a signature board. A signature board has the name of the

A Different Kind of Deck

Not everyone wants to jump through the air over obstacles and master the newest, gnarliest tricks. Some skateboarders just want to cruise along comfortably. If this is more your style, check out a longboard. They're longer than regular skateboards and wider, too. The wheels are really soft so you can glide over some pretty rough pavement. Interested? Look for longboards made by Sector 9, Gravity Streetboards, or Envy Skateboards.

Buying Your First Board: Two Perspectives

When buying a skateboard, there are usually two opinions on the subject: pre-assembled versus do-it-yourself. Andre Jarreau recommends that beginners take the pre-assembled route: "I recommend going out and getting one of those cheap boards for about $30. They're designed for the beginner. They come with bearings that aren't fast, which is good because you want to start slower. Going fast you get scared, and it's harder to do tricks fast."

Spencer Anthius, on the other hand, is a do-it-yourselfer. He is thirteen years old and started skating seven months ago. He says, "You want to have a good board when you're first starting because you want to have as much advantage as you can."

The choice is yours. If it feels like a hassle to pick out wheels and decks and trucks, don't worry. Just get a pre-assembled board. It doesn't have to be so complicated. Sometimes the most important thing is to just get started and have fun.

skater on the bottom and cool artwork. The most important thing is that the board feels right to you. It's your decision and your board.

Portable Art

For many people shopping for a deck, the best part is looking at all the cool skateboard art. It's hard to imagine decks without art on them, but twenty-five years ago most skate companies just put their names on the bottom of their boards. That changed in the late 1970s when a man named Wes Humpston started drawing designs on decks for his company, Dogtown Skates. His

The High Court of Skateboard Art

In the '80s, almost every skater had a skeleton or two lurking in his or her closet. You've probably seen the skeletons I'm talking about—a bony face peering out at you from a gaping hole in a T-shirt. Vernon "Court" Johnson created that face—and many of skating's most famous images—as the graphic artist for Powell Peralta. Tony Hawk's Screaming Skull design? Court did that. Steve Caballero's Dragon? Court did that too. Do you remember the Ripper—a skull tearing his way out of a ripped cloth? Yes, Court again! Powell Peralta produced thousands of stickers, T-shirts, posters, and boards with Court's designs on them. He took board art to a new level.

Skaters help create their own look and board identity using stickers, graffiti markers, even spray paint! Mirrors have been put on boards, and just about any kind of graphic design is possible. Being creative is not limited to how you ride.

boards jumped off the shelves and soon every other manufacturer jumped on the bandwagon. Skateboard decoration became a new art form.

Skateboard art today comes in almost every imaginable variety. Most board companies employ a full department of artists who produce new designs every year. If you want to make a statement with your board you can probably find the design that's a perfect fit. Some boards have demons and skulls while others have religious themes. With thousands of new boards coming out every year, the possibilities are endless.

Skate shops always carry a dizzying array of options when you are looking to buy a board that's right for you.

A Skater Speaks

Buying a board is no easy task. Daniel McLaughlin has been skating for six years and lives in Nashville, Tennessee. He shared his own board-buying experiences with us. Daniel makes sure that he has plenty of time to find the board that speaks to him. "I pick up every board in the shop," he says. "It just has to feel right. Some boards are wider than others, and they may have more or less concavity. You have to find what feels right to you. When I find the right board, I can feel the difference."

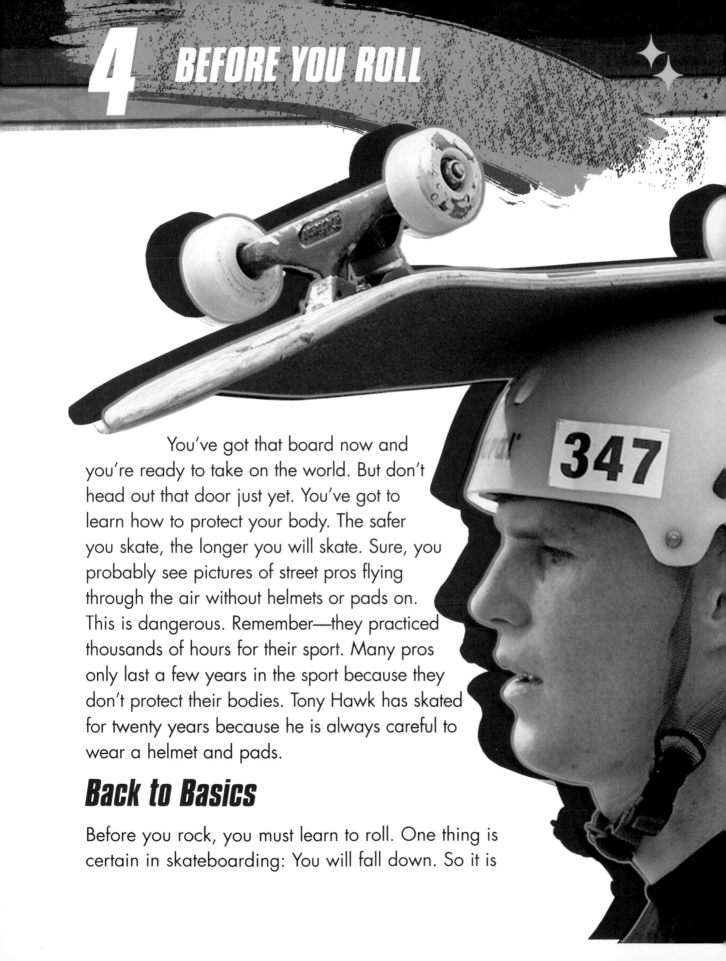

You've got that board now and you're ready to take on the world. But don't head out that door just yet. You've got to learn how to protect your body. The safer you skate, the longer you will skate. Sure, you probably see pictures of street pros flying through the air without helmets or pads on. This is dangerous. Remember—they practiced thousands of hours for their sport. Many pros only last a few years in the sport because they don't protect their bodies. Tony Hawk has skated for twenty years because he is always careful to wear a helmet and pads.

Back to Basics

Before you rock, you must learn to roll. One thing is certain in skateboarding: You will fall down. So it is

Skaters like Tony Hawk, who has taken literally thousands of spills over the years, have definitely benefited from helmets and elbow and knee pads.

important that you learn how to fall. Every fall is not the same. You can learn to fall in such a way that your body is protected. And you'll probably have fun learning. Practice first on a soft surface without your board. Lean your body toward the ground and roll forward. Keep your body loose as you roll forward in a somersault motion. Roll until your body comes to a stop naturally.

As you're getting used to the flexibility and balance of your board, take a few moments to practice this exercise: Place your board on some carpet or a gym mat. Make sure your feet are parallel, and just work on your balance. Rock gently in all directions and get used to the feel of your body on the board. This simple exercise can save you a few falls once you take to the street.

Perfect Protection

Any time you step on that board, you must protect yourself. A board with wheels is an unstable object. There are a few essential things that a skater must wear for protection. These are kneepads, elbow pads, and a helmet. And every beginner should also wear wrist guards. Whenever you wipe out, your hands extend instinctively to break your fall. Wrist guards will prevent a sprain, and you'll enjoy more time on the board rather than on the couch.

Cool or Uncool?

When it comes to wearing safety gear, some skaters worry that they won't look cool with pads and a helmet on. Some complain that bulky pads get in the way. But if you hang around a skatepark long enough you'll see that the ones who are still skating are the ones who know how to protect themselves. Andre Jarreau put it this way: "I used to have this argument of 'they get in the way,' but the more I bang up my knees and scrape my elbows, the more I realize that they're going to only help you. What gets in the way more, a bulky pad or a broken bone or a big swollen elbow?"

Get Your Gear On!

Safety gear is now one of the fastest growing areas in skateboard equipment sales.

Helmets and wrist guards are crucial in protecting you from serious injuries.

When skaters first started strapping on pads in the 1970s, there were no pads designed specifically for them. They had to wear pads designed for volleyball and other sports. Then, in 1977, skate pads finally hit the market. Skaters had one obvious choice—Rector pads. Today several additional companies make high-quality pads. Check out gear from TSG, Pro-Tec, Harbinger, or Pro-Designed.

If you're skating on ramps you'll quickly learn the art of the knee slide. You should get kneepads with a hard plastic outer shell. Rector and TSG both make good models. When you flame out on a ramp you can slide down to the bottom on your knees, safe and sound. It might wear out your shoes from rubbing the tips along the ramp surface, but your body will thank you.

Keeping Your Head on Straight

The most important piece of safety equipment is a good helmet. Whether you're on a vert ramp or the street, a helmet is essential for protection. Make sure your helmet is approved by the CPSC, the U.S. Consumer Product Safety Commission. They test gear to make sure it's safe. If you see their seal of approval on a helmet box you know you're in good hands.

Helmets actually do look pretty cool these days. Some pros have their own endorsed models. Tony Hawk and Mike Vallely both have signature helmets made by TSG, while Danny Way and Colin McKay protect their heads with CAPIX helmets. Look for a helmet from these companies—TSG, CAPIX, Element, or Pro-Tec. They all make high-quality helmets.

Andre says, "I just remember hitting my head one time in six years of skateboarding. I had a little ramp and I had probably been skating for about a year. I rolled up it and my wheels slipped and I just came crashing down on my head. That was not a pleasant experience—I saw stars, I felt like I was going to throw up, and I got dizzy. Head injuries are not fun. I'd rather lose my hand. Seriously."

Skate Fashion

Skateboarders have always been known for their unique sense of style. In the '90s, skateboard fashion became more mainstream than it had ever been before. Schools even tried to outlaw baggy pants! You don't have to wear super baggy pants to enjoy skateboarding, and you don't have to wear a certain brand. You just want to make sure that you are comfortable and flexible whenever you skate. Thirteen-year-old Spencer Anthius, who has skated for a little less than a year, shared his thoughts on skate clothes, saying, "People like to skate their own style. Some like loose pants and some like baggy pants. It's just kind of a fashion thing. Skate shirts, they look cool and everything, but they don't help you at all. I've never seen people judge how good a skater is by what they wear." Useful or not, skaters do have their

Skate style can encompass any number of fashions, including notoriously baggy pants.

favorite brands of clothes. Some of the favorites are Fourstar, Innes, TSA, Supernatural, NC Clothing, and Aesthetics.

Skate Shoes

It may not matter what brand of pants or shirts you wear when you skate, but if you're going to spend a lot of time skating you should probably get a pair of skateboard shoes. Regular tennis shoes or running shoes aren't made to take the constant abuse of skateboarding. If you're learning a new trick, you may fall or slide on your shoes a hundred times in one day. Skate shoes won't fall apart on you, and they are designed to keep your feet stable on the board. There are many brands and styles to choose from.

Some of the most popular brands include Axion, CIRCA, DC Shoes, Duffs, Emerica, ES, Etnies, Globe, Vans, Airwalk, DVS, and Lakai.

Once you have the board you want, take a long look at it, because it won't look this good for long. Once you start skating, that perfect paint finish will be scratched and scuffed in no time.

You probably want to keep riding as long as you can. Just like a favorite pair of shoes, many skaters have a favorite board. That means you have to learn how to take care of it. To maintain your board you'll need a few basic tools.

Essential Tools

There are five basic tools that every skateboarder should have.

1. Wheel wrench — 9/16"
2. Truck wrench — 1/2"
3. Hardware wrench — 3/8"
4. Phillips-head screwdriver
5. Allen wrench set

Keeping a skate wrench in your pocket lets you make repairs on the fly.

Luckily for you, there's no need to go skating around with all these tools jangling around in your pocket. If you want something that can fix most any problem, several companies make nifty skate tools that look a lot like a Swiss Army knife. They have several sizes of wrench and screwdriver heads, and will fix most roadside jams in a jiffy. Alien Workshop, Unit, Pig, and Shorty's all make one, as do other companies. They're small enough to slip in your pocket, and you can adjust your board on the fly. Any time you're out skating for a while you should stop periodically and check your board. Check the bolts and see if any are loose. You can fix your ride in a flash with your skate tool.

Spencer Anthius is a board expert after only seven months on wheels. He says, "I have some Allen wrenches and some skate tools. Skate tools are really helpful. You take them when you're street skating, put them in your pocket, and they fit right there. I do all of the work on my board. You learn as you go."

Troubleshooting

Check your mounting hardware periodically to make sure that everything's tight. Mounting hardware is all the nuts and bolts that hold your trucks on the deck.

Got some grit or mud in your grip tape? No problem. Just scrub it out with a bristly brush and a little water. Don't use a lot of water, though, because you don't want to waterlog your board.

How about those wheels? Give them a spin and make sure they turn easily. If you hear any noise there may be some dirt or grit in the bearings. And if one wheel spins while the other side is stuck you have a case of axle slip. This is pretty common when you try to kickflip and miss the landing. The axle slips over and jams one of the wheels in place. Hopefully you'll have your skate tools in your pocket. Otherwise you can whack it back into place against the sidewalk. But this isn't very healthy for the board or for you.

Stressed Out

After taking a beating day in and day out, stress cracks start to appear in the board around the base of the trucks. The pressure of your body landing on the board starts to crack the wood over time. When this happens, it's time to start looking for a new board. You can still skate on it for a while, but stress cracks signal the beginning of the end for a deck.

Stress cracks are normal, but there are a few things you can do to slow down this process. First, remember to land directly over your trucks every time. The trucks help absorb the pressure of your landing. It's very common for skaters to snap off the backs of their boards when landing with their feet behind the trucks after a big jump. Second, consider investing in riser pads. Riser pads fit in between the trucks and the deck and cushion your landing impact. This will help lengthen the life of your board. They do add a little height to your board, and you'll have to see how that feels for you.

Tony Hawk's equipment from an X Games competition really shows how skating can wear down a board.

The trucks will eventually wear out, too, especially if you're grinding them a lot doing street tricks. Replace the bushings when they get squashed and flattened from countless landings.

Nose slides and tail slides wear out the ends of the board, and the layers of wood (the plies) may begin to separate. As your board cracks or wears out, you'll get less "pop" in your jumps.

Sometimes board maintenance calls for creative solutions. Andre Jarreau shared one of his stories with us: "The most interesting thing I've done with a stress crack is I took carpenter's glue, I fingered the plies and separated them, then I squirted in a whole mess of glue. I ripped the grip tape off so the deck was bare. Then

Stars and Their Gear

Professional skateboarders can trade in their boards if they start to wear out. Most pro skaters make their money and their living from sponsorships. Companies pay skaters to use their products when they skate. So pros get paid and they get loads of free gear. They get everything from stickers to boards to shoes. Here are some pro skaters and the gear they use. As you'll notice, all of these skaters have excelled at their sport using very different equipment. It's not what you skate, but how you skate.

Tony Hawk
Deck: Birdhouse
Helmet: TSG
Shoes: Hawk Shoes

Mike Vallely
Wheels: Accel Wheels
Helmet: TSG
Shoes: Etnies
Bearings: Speed Metal

Eric Koston
Deck: Girl
Trucks: Royal
Clothes: Fourstar
Shoes: eS

Jamie Thomas
Deck: Zero
Trucks: Mercury
Wheels: Pig
Hardware: Shorty's
Clothes: Innes
Shoes: Adio

When it comes to making skating fun and keeping it that way, safety is definitely the top priority.

I clamped it down and I held it there for a day. When I came back it was stronger than it was before and it wasn't about to fall apart. That was important for me because I couldn't get any boards at the time. I didn't have any money; I was in seventh grade."

Now That You're Ready . . .

It's time to go out and have fun! That's the most important thing to remember as you take a spin on your new wheels. First and foremost, skateboarding is about having fun. Just remember to be safe and protect your body so you will be skating for many years to come.

GLOSSARY

base plate The portion of the trucks that attaches to the underside of the skateboard.

bushings Small rubber pieces that fit on the kingpin and help in turning (also called pivot bushings).

concave The amount of upward curve on the sides of a skateboard deck.

Consumer Products Safety Commission (CPSC) A United States government regulatory agency that tests products for safety.

diameter Thickness or width.

durometer An instrument used to measure the hardness of urethane wheels.

hangar The part of the trucks that contains the axle. You grind on the hangar.

kingpin The bolt on the trucks that connects the hangar to the base plate.

riser pads Rubber spacers used between the trucks and the board.

urethane The plastic compound used to make modern skateboard wheels.

vert Flying straight up in the air with help from ramps with high sides; short for "vertical" skating.

FOR MORE INFORMATION

Organizations

California Amateur Skateboard
   League (CASL)
P.O. Box 30004
San Bernadino, CA 92413
(909) 883-6176
Web site: http://www.caslusf.com/

International Association of Skateboard Companies (IASC)
P.O. Box 37
Santa Barbara, CA 93116
(805) 683-5676
Web site: http://www.skateboardiasc.org

United Skateboarding Association
P.O. Box 986
New Brunswick, NJ 08903
(732) 432-5400 ext. 2168 or 2169
Web site: http://www.unitedskate.com

Magazines

Transworld Skateboarding
TransWorld Media
353 Airport Road
Oceanside, CA 92054
(760) 722-7777
Web site: http://www.skateboarding.com

Skateboarder
33046 Calle Aviador
San Juan Capistrano, CA 92675
Web site: http://www.skateboardermag.com

Web Sites

Due to the changing nature of Internet links, the Rosen Publishing Group, Inc., has developed an online list of Web sites related to the subject of this book. This site is updated regularly. Please use this link to access the list:

http://www.rosenlinks.com/wsk/cbss/

FOR FURTHER READING

Brooke, Michael. *The Concrete Wave: The History of Skateboarding.* Toronto: Warwick Publishing, 2000.

Burke, L.M. *Skateboarding! Surf the Pavement.* New York: Rosen Publishing, 1999.

Gould, Marilyn. *Skateboarding.* Mankato, MN: Capstone Press, 1991.

Powell, Ben. *Extreme Sports: Skateboarding.* Hauppauge, NY: Barron's Educational Series, 1999.

Ryan, Pat. *Extreme Skateboarding.* Mankato, MN: Capstone Press, 1998.

Shoemaker, Joel. *Action Sports: Skateboarding Streetstyle.* Mankato, MN: Capstone Press, 1995.

Werner, Doug. *Skateboarder's Start-up: 14 Tricks You Should Know.* Chula Vista, CA: Start-up Sports/Tracks Publishing, 2000.

BIBLIOGRAPHY

Bob's Trick Tips. Retrieved November 10, 2001 (http://www.bobstricktips.com).

Brooke, Michael. *The Concrete Wave: The History of Skateboarding*. Toronto: Warwick Publishing, 2000.

Mike Vallely.com. Retrieved November 10, 2001 (http://www.mikevallely.com).

Skateboard.com. Retrieved November 10, 2001 (http://www.skateboard.com).

Skateboard Science. Retrieved November 10, 2001 (http://www.exploratorium.edu/skateboarding/skatedesign.html).

Tony Hawk.com. Retrieved November 10, 2001 (http://www.tonyhawk.com).

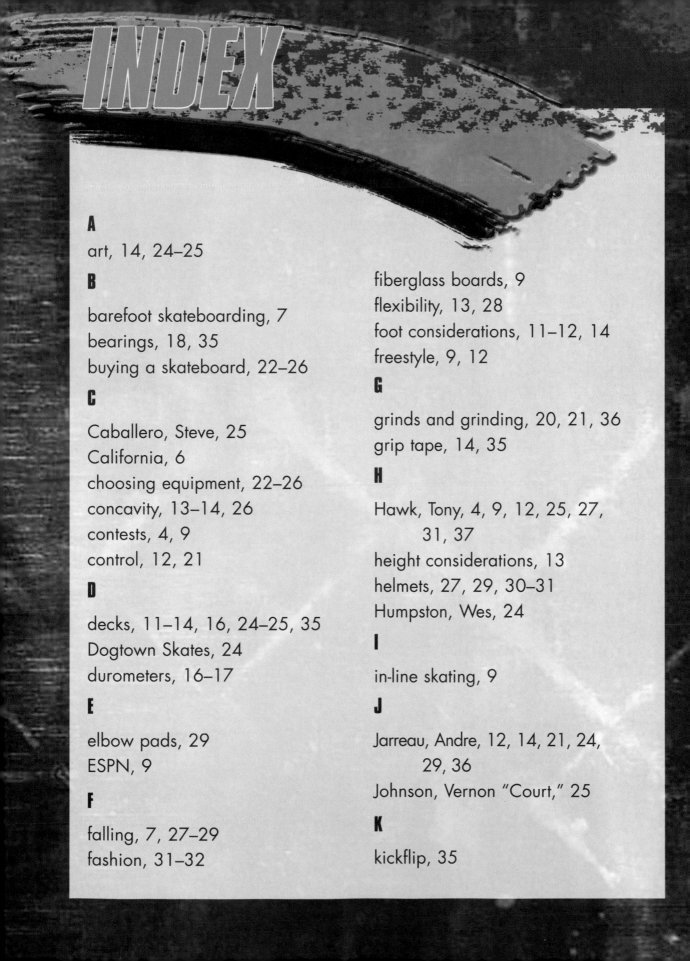

INDEX

CREDITS

About the Author

Brian Wingate got his first skateboard when he was twelve. After trying unsuccessfully to become a skateboard superstar, he removed the wheels and used the deck as a snowboard. His love for adventure and learning has led him all over the world. He now lives in Tennessee with his wife and daughter.

Photo Credits

Editor

Mark Beyer

Design and Layout

Thomas Forget